Lyn

Thanks for
coming to
the
retreat.

Cyal
Bar

ROOTED

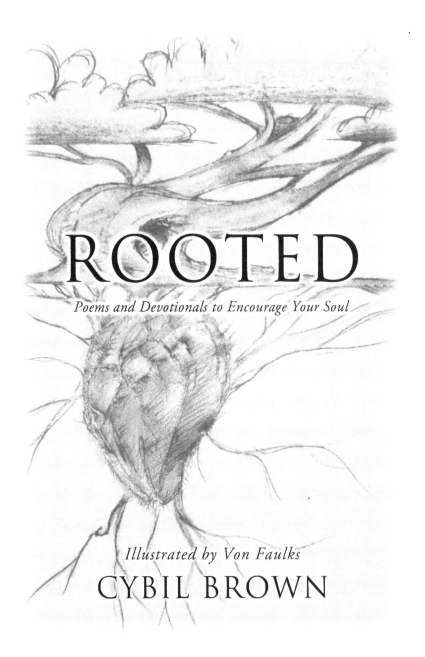

ROOTED

Poems and Devotionals to Encourage Your Soul

Illustrated by Von Faulks

CYBIL BROWN

XULON PRESS

Xulon Press
2301 Lucien Way #415
Maitland, FL 32751
407.339.4217
www.xulonpress.com

Paperback ISBN-13: 978-1-66287-966-1
Ebook ISBN-13: 978-1-66287-967-8

Dedication

This book is dedicated to fellow writer, William Ward, and First Lady Thelma Gilliam. You both were very inspiring and challenged me to publish my work. May you both continue to RIH

To the first dude I ever loved, Willie Mack Patterson, aka my daddy. Rest easy, big guy.

Anything worth building. Anything worth sharing,
Anything truly everlasting is deeply rooted in Jesus Christ.
Von Faulks, Illustrator

Preface

Proverbs 3:18 (CSB):She (Wisdom) is a tree of life to those who embrace her and those who hold on to her are happy.

Matthew 12:33 (CSB): A tree is known by its fruit.

Jeremiah 17:8 (CSB): They will be like a tree planted by the water that sends out its roots by stream. It does not fear when heat comes; its leaves are always green. It has no worries in a year of drought and never fails to bear fruit.

I believe I am a deeply rooted tree, ready to embrace new situations. However, there are times when God literally had to pluck me up because I became too comfortable or compromised to fit Him in. I am quick to get stuck in a mindset or state of being because I feel like I am in control. I get into a rhythm and a flow.

Sometimes I am just resistant to growth and change. Stretching produces a push beyond our cozy zones of predictability. Growth often hurts and requires a deep look inside — self-reflection that is so raw and honest that you don't recognize yourself in the mirror.

Introduction

M y middle name is Latrice, But my family calls me "trea" pronounced "tree" for short. The Bible has distinct characteristics of trees:

- A metaphor for wisdom
- Is known by its fruit.
- Is planted.

If you Google the word rooted, you find adjectives and verbs, such as established deeply, embedded, formed, ingrained, and developed.

Being called "Trea" is a term of affection and endearment, especially when it came from my mom, Aunt Tine, or my cousin Cake Cake yelling, "Cybil Latrice!" There is just something about family that will forever be etched in our memory. My family from P-Town (Portsmouth, Virginia) have always supported me and have my back, whether it was mother's side or my dad's side of the family in the blue house on the corner in New Towne. I have always felt supported. My favorite color is green and has been as long as I can remember. To me it represents life, renewing, and springtime. My wedding colors were green and brown. See a theme here?

Even when I left my sheltered and protected nest, God blessed me with wonderful peers and a lifelong mentor at

Virginia Commonwealth University. Richmond exposed me to a range of diversity and experiences like literature readings that 'caused my brain to explode with ideas, concepts, and never-spoken-out-loud perspectives. Outside of my family, I connected with others and felt a part of a community. They understood my nerdy love of books, my faith, and my need to discover myself.

As I entered the workforce, I met co-workers who embraced me and supervisors who would challenge and sometimes nearly break me. They have held my hand through career changes, marriage, and motherhood. They have become great friends and mentors. I have laughed with fellow writers and enjoyed the spoken word stage. I've had small parts in church plays that allowed me to unleash the drama mama. Even up until marriage and motherhood, I have been deeply loved and firmly planted. To put it simply, I have been rooted!

Contents

Part 1: Poetry

College Days

That's All

To hold you in the springtime and kiss you in the fall.
To feel your heart and mine dance
That's all I want; that's all.

To think of you when I awake
And dine you in my dreams.
To love you completely all over.
That's all I want; that's all

To sprinkle you with pure magic
That makes your smile glow
to see the sunrise in your eyes.
That's all I want; that's all

To understand all the difficult times
And give you the space you need
To wipe away all those tears
That's all I want; that's all.

To take away the stress and pain
Give God's promise of peace.
To assure what we have will last
That's all I want; that's all.

Sister-Friend

You are my sister-friend; you build me up.
I help you maintain when life is so rough.
We have a spiritual connection that's so rare.
Lord, thank you for blessing me with them.
They recharge my smile when it's dim.
Empathize as tears run down my face.
My funky mood 'causes them to give me space.
Tough love is given when I am wrong.
After being put in my place, they're gonna have a testimony service on the phone.
Sometimes we gossip 'cause we think we grown.
I couldn't make it without these angels on earth.
You knew I would need them before my birth.
Thank you for your sisterhood Paulette and Roshon.

Scared Early

He touched me, and he knew he wasn't right.
I was totally shocked and didn't think to fight.
How could this happen to me? I didn't do anything.
I was just a child, and we didn't have a fling.
He was a family friend, and I trusted him with my life.
But the truth in looking back, I wish I'd had a knife.
He died not long after that on the path to my aunt's house.
Basically since that day, I've been quiet as a mouse.
Until now, cause young girls need to know.
That your yes means yes and your no means no
Never let any man disrespect you or your body.
Even if he buys you nice things or calls you a hottie.
Your body is a temple and deserves appropriate affection.
You want a mature man with a spiritual connection.
Never let your self-esteem be deflated by what one man has done.
God loves you so much, and
His radiance is reflected by His Son.
Don't let your guilt from the
past ruin your destiny
You are a queen, and your prince is waiting
He wants what's best for thee.

UPS, Yes!

Lord, send me a good Christian man.
Intelligent, funny, and who would understand.
That You are first in my life.
I'm not rushing to be a wife.
I'll pay for postage, shipping, and handling.
He doesn't need a big bank account, car, ring,
Just a desire to love You more and more.
He will be a cutie, I'm sure.
Whenever, Jesus, you're ready to ship.
Whomever You sent, and I promise—no lip.
You always know what I need, Lord.
I'll pray and be faithful in one accord with him, wherever
he may be,
I promise to handle with care, you'll see.

Living Epistles

An epistle is a poem or literary work which is in the form of a letter or series of letters. God blessed my family with two beautiful grandmothers who lived their lives like a love story to us. I grew up thinking they would live forever and would sew my wedding dress.

Mary Johnson was a frisky grandmother who fed the neighborhood and healed anyone my cousin "Pop" brought to her. She cooked us a hot breakfast every day before school and started Sunday dinner the night before. She made you laugh with her "Mr. Good bar" joke. She loved to watch her soap operas, Wheel of Fortune, and to observe her family enjoying her cooking. She would help anyone in need. At her funeral, I described her as our family's grace despite the thorns we faced. I joked that she was in heaven at a buffet line and peeping under an angel's wings.

Ella Bell was consummate baker and a prayer warrior. She took a curtain and made a dress for my cousin Kim for church. She liked to go fishing and questioned wrestlers' body odor in the WWE. She accepted every grandchild's high school and college graduation invitation with the help of my Uncle Chris. During her memorial, I discussed her unwavering faith and her positive impact on those who knew her. Despite her limited education, she taught herself to read the Bible with the assistance of Uncle JL. She was always humming some gospel tune. These two ladies lived across the street from one another and viewed each other as sisters. They had sung in the choir and ushered together at a COGIC church.

How lucky I was to have them in my life for so long. They were the best grandmothers any grandchild could have. I will always remember and continue their legacy of love, family, faith, and cooking until I see them again.

Help Me Stay

I like to watch cartoons and lick batter from the cake bowl.
One day, I'll have a car and go to college; that's my goal.
But for now, I'm gonna enjoy just being a kid.
Although I don't get to do it much, I wish I could.

See, my family sometimes curses and gets tipsy around me.
I come downstairs, and they may have a porn on TV.
They send me to purses to get out smokes.
I've even seen some of my cuz's sniff some dope.

What happened to the time when I stayed in my place?
Played board games and Nintendo instead of being on Myspace
When the streetlights came on and I was in the house,
Grown folks having a discussion and I'm quiet as a mouse.

I went to church every Sunday 'cause it wasn't an option.
And I gladly took what Mommy brought when we went
shopping. If I didn't follow directions, out to get a switch, I went.
You better not complain to your teacher—not even a hint.

Please, family, help me stay in my place, please.
Acting like I'm older is toxic like a disease.
Let me enjoy the few years I have in childhood.
I don't want to ever look back and wish I could!

IF, When, Then

IF you truly love her, tell her When you get a chance.
Then mean it when you say it.
IF she is the apple of your life, kiss her
When nights are cold.
Then she will reciprocate

IF you desire her soft caresses, seek to please her When you touch,
Then bring to life fantasies.
IF her opinions really matter, listen carefully When she speaks.
Then she'll tell you all her secrets
IF you're secure in the relationship, you will not worry When fellas come around.
Then trust can be the foundation of what you are building
IF you respect her holy temple
When sex does not follow a passionate kiss, Then God blesses you both.
IF she is the love of your life, and compliments are plenty When you speak of her,
Then communication is made easy
IF you never want her to leave, you'll think of your mother When treating her like an angel.
Then love can last forever.

Moody

Lord, why is it that I praise Your name
Only when things are great, and I gain?
You have done so much for me.
With every blessing, I should reverence Thee.
But when life gets a little too thick, I hide; no prayer or
faith, I split.
Only negative works and thoughts do I have Walking by what
I see, am I really saved?
For it is the devil's plan to throw me off track.
Every time I get things under control, he comes with a smack!
The Word says I'm more than a conqueror in Christ He died for
my sins; no one else but Him, a sacrifice.
His love for me is unconditional and free,
but I feel I don't deserve it, you see,
for I don't always feel like doing the things I should, But God
is so much stronger than me, I could.
It's He who truly lives and rules on the inside.
And my behavior should reflect this on the outside the devil
only has power that I give him.
And in God's eyesight, I am a victorious gem. I can accomplish
any obstacle, every time, Submitting to Him at the drop
of a dime.
So, the next time I feel a bad mood coming on.

I'll just put on my Walkman and a song. I'm glad, Jesus, you have never left me yet.

Every time I call, you answer, that's a bet.

Please, Lord, forgive me for not putting You first and thanks for not being moody like me or worse. Help me to delight myself in You always.

And wherever I am, I will continue to stay. Allow peace to enter my heart in troubled times Let laughter meet my fears even when I find That there is no possible escape provided.

And have no other options the world has decided.

I will continue to trust in You and be forever grateful.

Knowing that You will deliver me—Mr. Faithful

Hide and Seek

He that findeth a wife findeth a good thang. But I'm here standing. Can somebody please explain? Am I too holy, desperate, or too deep to have a man to share my heart? Maybe I should leave it alone and give it to God right from the start?

Help me, God, to stay busy and focus my love on You. You know my desires and my heart.

When you're ready You will send me a boo, I want a three-string chord with You, Lord, right in the middle and at my wedding, we will sing with the cat on the fiddle.

I Don't Worry When I Am with You

The world stops when you walk in. My man, my boo but mostly my friend.

And when we play, no way do I delay celebrating and enjoy one year in May.

I know that when we sleep, the sheets stay on. Not trying to set up scenes from a porn.

God's holy temple is a strong tower Only He has the mercy, grace, and power.

To sustain us to be His chosen few

As He cleanses us through and through

You are a perfect gentleman, honoring my wishes.

As I continually reward you with kisses.

Your boyish smile makes me blush.

And when you enter the room, everyone is hushed.

Healing

Since you've been gone,
I've been trying to hold on.
Looks like all I do is cry.
Feels like something inside has died.
Maybe our breakup was for the best.
Now I realize that I am blessed.
I don't have to beg you to stay.
True love is soon to come my way.
I need to move on and get over you.
If the script was flipped, that's what you would do

Don't want to stay stuck in the past.
The future is unclear like a clouded glass.
I made you responsible for my happiness.
Only God gives joy to His vessels a real test.
I've enjoyed all the good times we shared.
No one wants to be hurt again and again.
Life is about risks—some loses some wins.
My heart has healed through time.
I've learned to forgive a dime.

Experience is good teacher to me.
With Jesus and the Holy Spirit, that makes three.
There's nothing in the world I can't handle.

My hurts were on blast like a scandal.
Self-care is important and brings me nearer
To my purpose to encourage and uplift others
To run this race and be a finisher.

A Second Chance

Yeah, she messed up, and you know what she did. She got pregnant with no husband and had a kid. But things are different now 'cause she got saved.

She is on the straight and narrow road to heaven that is paved. She is a new creature in Christ, and the old has passed away. She dedicated me back to the Lord; man, what a great day.

Please do not hate on my mom 'cause I love her so much.

With you in her life will add a special touch. See she has been through the playas and thugs. After all that drama, feeling less than mud.

She needs a godly man in her life to lead like a lion.

But nurturing enough to love her like a lamb.

Will you man up and step to the plate?

Tell my mom how you feel before it is too late!

All Over

Sweet, passionate, gentle yet strong—kisses Kisses, kisses, kisses all over.

Desirablesoft, teasing, and unforgettable—touches Touches, touches, touches all over.

Quiet, mysterious, sexy yet distracting—glances Glances, glances, glances all over

Protective, yet shy, confident and demanding—love Love, love, love all over.

Quality, peaceful, enjoyable, with you—time Time, time, time all over

Seductive, powerful, exotic yet playful—whispers, Whispers, whispers, whispers all over.

Unique, handsome, mature, and hardworking- you You, you, you all over.

I want, cherish, admire and love- my man My man, my man, my man all over.

Lonely, Help Lord

Jesus is all the man I need.
Yet in me society has sown a seed
I can't possibly be happy without a brother
Who will love, and care like to no other.
But when you chart your own course of life.
His will is ruled out and you experience strife.
God has a perfect plan for us all to fulfill.
So, if a mate is in order, don't worry; just chill,
It's not a sin to want to have a special buddy.
Eve had Adam, and we all came from some puddy.

Forget Jesus

God is good all the time!
And all the time God is good!
This phrase is a popular one heard
in many churches on Sunday morning. I wonder if people really
know about His goodness. We get married in
churches that represent a new beginning or endeavor in which
we ask God to bless.
Our children are christened before Him to "sanctify" a new life
that needs His presence
presence. We sat in the temple the day after that unforgettable
Tuesday in September to ask God why and to redeem lost souls.
Can He find us once situations and events are resolved? We
seem to seek His face only when we need Him.
But our relationship with Him deserves daily contact. We build
intimacy in other relationships by spending time and talking
forever. We need to meet God with that same energy and desire.
The Lord longs for us to enter His presence. However, we only
enter like a convenience store for quick drive-through blessings.

Lord, Have Mercy

He's my teddy bear, and he has the sweetest smile.

When he looks at me, I blush; make me wanna travel miles Just to see his face and feel secure in his arms.

He wins me over when I'm mad with his charm, and it happened so quickly one night.

He kissed my lips, and I resisted—yeah right!

His laugh sneaks up on you like a child playing hide and seek.

He's compassionate, gentle, humble, spoiled, and kinda meek.

Don't tell him I told you 'cause he a lil' shy.

Got me trippin like Johnny saying, "My, My, My!"

Detour

I want your heart, but you gave me your body instead.
I love your kisses and your touch, but ain't much talking in bed.
See, I need to connect with you on a much deeper level.
You are part of me cause God used your rib; that is clever.
Do not be afraid to let your guard down and be free.
At times, my life seems so empty, but with you, it will not be.
So, turn this ship around and let us go full throttle.
We got something special, and I can be your genie in a bottle.

The Box

In my mind, I have an "ideal" man.
Tall, dark, and handsome, that is the plan.
My knowledge of Christ would grow because of him.
Hs covenant with family is stronger than his boys and them.
His leadership skills are on point, and he is gentle as a lamb.
My needs always coming first with respect—no scam!
Low-key, shy, nerdy yet prolific,
A great kisser, dancer, and cook, just terrific.
Just the kind of man my mom would like, My prince in shining
armor, my black knight.

Then you show up and snatch the nails out my box. You flip
the script, got me running crazy like a fox. You are nothing I
ever expected to come my way, from the beginning, I doubted
"us" and had to pray but you will not let me go, and you have
made it clear.
You challenge my mind, heart, and soul, so sincere.
I see myself in a whole new light because of you and even if I
did not say, I appreciate what you do.
I feel grown, alive, and sexy in your presence. Forever in my
book, you go down as a legend!

Held Hostage

I was held hostage in a relationship that did not exist. Time went so fast; my mind was in a twist.

We made plans to attend concerts and watch favorite shows.

You didn't give us a chance, and what the future held, who knows.

You pursued me at the Wawa up the street; you liked my hat, said it was sweet. We had a couple of fun dates and some deep conversations.

Things were moving along, and I felt elevation.

To something deeper and more permanent, but your parents were divorcing, and you were mentally turbulent.

You went MIA for a period of time.

Keeping me safe, out of sight on the sideline. You needed a friend more than you wanted a girl.

Don't waste my time because I am a true pearl.

Part 2: Devotionals

Blind Faith

An Unwanted Blessing

Romans 8:28 (CSB)
"We know that all things work together for
the good of those who love the God, who are
called according to His purpose."

You ever have an argument with God? Well, I've had quite a few, and guess who lost the debates every time? Sometimes I just don't see how the "all things" is working for my good. Back in November of 2002, I was forced to seek out a counselor at church. Days before, a seventeen-year-old boy snatched my purse off my shoulder along with my sense of peace and control. Do you know what it's like to not be able to sleep or jump when someone approaches you? Everyone who looks at you or comes near is guilty without a trial. How dare this happen to me? I was the good church girl who paid her tithes and looked out for her friends. I was loyal, dependable, and had a good sense of humor. Why me, Lord?

And God answered and said, "Why not you? You are no better than any of my creations. You have to go through this in order to get to the next level." I walked away with my head down like a child in my preschool class sent to time-out. The only difference is I didn't know how long it was going to last.

My counselor helped me deal with the anxiety, bitterness, and guilt I felt I had the right to transfer to the robber. Let's not forget the unsolicited advice I received from people were in the same situation. Some people were so blunt without an ounce of respect or empathy. In retrospect, I realize the young man did what he reasoned he needed to do to get what he wanted. Through counseling, I learned to let God handle my inconvenience and frustrations as I gained a new appreciation for life and for those who work in the judicial system.

The "all things" is important if we just pay attention. I did not get hurt, even though the teen claimed he would shoot me. The two dollars in my purse, the carbon-copied checks, denied ATM card, store manager, police officer church member, counselor, and my memory all worked for my good.

I have a beautiful testimony. I received my purse back, and the young man was picked up the same night of the robbery. My counselor went to court with me both times and continues to be a resource even today. Sad to see, the teen was found guilty and had to serve three years for my two dollars.

Life is not fair, and people can be cruel. But I am thankful to know that God was with me all the time. He had a wonderful plan to restore and redeem my life. I am more valuable to Him than my purse. I praise Him that I survived the attack. He gave me the patience, peace, and words to say in court. I am more observant of my surroundings when I'm out in public. I can now help others be victorious and not just a random victim.

When I was younger, I used to wonder what I had done to bring bad things on myself. Now I know that God is in control of the good and bad. Matthew 5:45 states, He sends rain on the unrighteous and righteous." Everyone likes to receive blessings, but few like the packaging. UPS has no mandate on heaven's deliveries. God desires loading docks in your humble heart.

Handle with prayer!

Policy and Procedures

John 14:15 If you love Me, keep My commandments.

Hebrew 4:12 For the word of God is living and powerful and sharper than any two-edged sword, piercing even to the division of soul and spirit, and of joints and marrow, and is a discerner of the thoughts and intents of the heart.

M ost of us Type A personalities are compliant at work. We want to walk the line and be seen as competent. In addition, we have a nice flare of flexibility and laidback-ness, if that's a word. When you hear about a new policy at work, what is your typical reaction? Do you roll your eyes and sigh? Do you smile with joy because the new procedure was your recommendation? Do you grin in your supervisor's face, secretly knowing you will not do what was asked? Policies and procedures are just standards that add organization and guidelines to a company. With that being said, what does the Bible offer to you?

There are many metaphors that have been attached to the Bible, such as roadmap, guidepost, or instruction manual. In reality, it is all those things. Just like company policy, we must look at the big picture. A person's background and experience with their former supervisor or company paints their perception of what has been asked of them. Like company policies, the Bible is not open for discussion or debate. So, why do we not waste time to comply with company rules but not the Bible? Jesus came to give us life more abundantly. The Word is a light unto our path. Dr. Bill Winston, Senior Pastor of Living Word Christian Center said "The Bible is not about opinions but the Kingdom of God" during a camp meeting at FaithLandmark Ministries on October 09, 2022. God's way of doing things often goes against our flesh. God disciplines those who He loves. Whether it is negative feedback from our supervisor, natural parent, or heavenly Father, it does not always feel good.

It's easy to take instructions from a tangible boss who signs a tangible check for you every two weeks. That check is based on your performance and understood expectations.

Cousin Johnny

Then Jesus comes from Galilee to John at the
Jordan, to be baptized by him. But John tried
to stop him, saying, "I need to be baptized by
you, and yet you come to me?

Matthew 11: 2–3 (CSB)
Now when John heard in prison what the
Christ was doing, he sent a messenger through
his disciples and asked him "Are you the
one who is to come, or should we except
someone else?"

Luke 1:41 (CSB)
When Elizabeth heard Mary's greeting, the
baby leaped inside her, and Elizabeth was
filled with the Holy Spirit.

J esus and John the Baptist were cousins. John was only six
months older than his cousin. The Scriptures tell us that
Jesus grew in favor, wisdom, and stature. We also know that
He did not begin His ministry until He was thirty years old. He
spent years in preparation before God gave him His platform to
serve. Were these cousins not aware of each other's ministries
over the years?

Indeed, they were. Johnny understood that he was preparing the way for Jesus, although his methods were radical. Are you living your life that your cousins would want to follow Christ? Are you an example of God's blessings but also His victory through trials? When you walk into a room, are you bringing peace or drama? Our first ministry is to our household and our loved ones.

Speak Now or Forever . . .

Mark 8:38 (NIV)
If anyone is ashamed of me and my words
in this adulterous and sinful generation, the
Son of Man will be ashamed of them when
he comes in his Father's glory with the
holy angels.

In the fall of 1996, I was on my way to VCU after spending a weekend at home in Tidewater. I ventured home like most college student for some home-cooked meals, free laundry, and shopping. My mom decided to take me back instead of me catching the bus like my original trip. Along with my mom were my two cousins, an aunt, and my grandmother.

As we started the journey to Richmond, I quietly prayed to myself for safety on the road. Even though I was raised in the church, I was nervous about speaking about God around certain people including my family. I tossed and turned trying to get comfortable enough for a nap in the last row of seats. Finally, I decided to take my seat belt off.

Outside of Williamsburg, Virginia, my mom started to swerve. The van shook, and I awoke disoriented to my surroundings. My family started to call my mom's name "Thomasine! Thomasine!" They yelled. I didn't know what was going on. I cried out "Oh Lord! Oh Lord!" We ran off the road and hit a tree. Every one of my family members went to the hospital in an ambulance except me and my two-year-old cousin. I rode up front with the paramedic.

My grandmothers always said that "God watches over fools and babies." My cousin was the baby, and I was the fool who took off my seat beat. The doctors ran an EKG test and numerous others on my mom but couldn't find a cause to her blacking out. My oldest cousins broke her one of her legs. My grandmother had broken ribs and sternum. My aunt broke her nose. My little cousin had a scrape on her nose, and I had a few on my left leg that remain to this day.

Later, I thanked God for protecting us. It could have been deadly. The van was totaled, yet my belongings—even my glasses—were not damaged. Many travelers stopped to help us. About a month later, my family traveled to that stretch of I-64 to find that the tree saved our lives. It was not there! When I heard that, I really began to cry.

So now when you see me speak about God, it's not to show off. Whether it's for God, children, parents, teachers, or you, I will speak. I don't have a closet religion. I have a relationship with Christ that I know is real. I will not be ashamed of who He is or what He has done for me. I am a child of the King. That's why my license plates read GZUSKID!

The Parent Trap

M any of us know about the classic movie that has been
redone about the twins who switch places.

> Deuteronomy 5:16 (CSB)
> Honor your father and mother, as the Lord
> your God commanded you, so that you may
> live long and that it may go well with you in
> the land the Lord your God is giving you.

Is it easier to honor them when you are a child or an adult?
When you are little, you idealize your parents. They are larger
than life. For the most part, they are your favorite people besides
your grandparents. They are the ones who ask you a trillion
questions, not really waiting for the answer before they move
on to the next question. There is a shift as children transition
to teens. They start listening to and depending on their peers
more than their parents. They stumble into adulthood like the
anxious toddler who just learned how to walk with no support,
wanting to be left alone but not mature enough to manage the
responsibility right now.

Parents often wonder where the time flies as these young
people move out starting careers and families. Parents observe
from afar the tough lessons their "kids" must learn. Despite
the rolled eyes and poked-out lips, they were listening. They

say they will never be like their parents, but some habits are unconsciously passed down. For some, a wonderful parent–adult child relationship develops. Parents must fight the need to give unwanted advice or bail them out financially every time. You can talk about things you never did before. This is a beautiful thing.

What happens when the parents become bitter, angry, or entitled?

> Ephesians 6:4 (CSB)
> Fathers do not exasperate your children;
> instead, bring them up in the training and
> instruction of the Lord.

The last part of the verse lets us know that Paul was talking about young children in the home. However, could the beginning portion refer to parents with their adult children? Have you ever experienced or witnessed someone's parents going off or giving attitude to their adult children? It's wild to experience or observe. I am not sure if it's entitlement, a loss of control, or fear of the unknown future, for your child's future, or wondering who will be there for you as you get older? Are they reflecting over their life, parenting choices, or regrets? What makes a parent treat an adult child so badly? What makes an adult child hang around? Is it obligation, fear, or just stubbornness?

Reading Rainbows

R ainbows are mesmerizing phenomenon to an especially curious child. Rainbows grab your attention despite what is going on around you. Perhaps this was the motivation for one of my favorite shows as a child, *Reading Rainbows*. Hosted by LaVar Burton, it promised to take you on a journey by inviting your imagination to escape by just opening a book.

In June, I found myself heading to my hometown to start my vacation. It was a mystical Friday with showers off and on. Outside of Hampton, Virginia, I encountered a huge, yet faint outline of a rainbow in the distance. As I drove closer, the colors seemed to jump out at me and radiate the sky. The highway no longer had my attention. The rainbow's bold presence and demanding intensity made me feel safe.

Leaving Hampton, I thought of the many dry spells in my Christian walk when I desired a rainbow or any sign of God's promises. He reminded of a few things that day in my car.

1. He is always closer than we think.
2. We can see crystal clear when we press into Him.
3. His will is more distinctive when He is our focus.
4. Concentrating on Him helps us ignore the clouds and darkness behind.
5. He is superior to any adversity or test we face.

6. Actual interactions with the Father redefine our reality and dispels assumptions.

The rainbow appeared after the storm. God is high on His throne and looks down low to all. The wonderful thing is that He created the rain and the storm. You don't need a psychic to predict your future. Ride out the storms in your life and meet Him at the end. Have you read your rainbow today?

Genesis 9:16 (NIV)
Whenever the rainbow appears in the clouds,
I will see it and remember the everlasting
covenant between God and all living creatures
of every kind on the earth.

You Never Told Me

So many people have opinions, especially when they are unsolicited. However, there are times when they should share useful information.

You never told me there would come a time when my husband and I would not like each other. That there would be moments when I felt like a failure concerning my children and career. It takes time to forgive yourself from past regrets and mistakes.

Unforgiveness keeps you bound mentally and emotionally paralyzes you. No one could ever convince me my closest friends would betray me.

I never knew what church hurt was until I was in tears or that your own family could dog you out behind your back.

Fear can keep you stuck in your tracks and negate your dreams. Every time you catch up with the Jones's, they move.

There will be times when you struggle to believe all God's promises are yes and amen.

My grandmothers' faith can't save me. I must have an authentic relationship with Christ.

When I surrender to Jesus, He shows me how to truly love my husband, be a prudent parent, navigate storms of life, and forgive all.

One Race, Our Peace

Ephesians 2:14–16
For He, our peace who made both groups one
and tore down the dividing wall of hostility.
So that He might create in Himself one new
man from two, resulting in peace. He did this
so that he might reconcile both to God in one
body through the cross by which he put their
hostility to death.

The above passage of Scripture clearly paints a world that sees each human being as a part of one race. Paul was talking about the Jews and the Gentiles, the circumcised versus the uncircumcised. Physical attributes, personalities, and mannerisms separate us. However, Jesus made Himself our peace, and those differences are not important. Each man is equal to the next man, and yet racism is alive in America.

I have a hard time wrapping my brain around how much Black and Brown people are hated so much. Like an unborn child who had no say so in his or her birth, no one gets to choose their race or ethnicity. We just want to live our lives and build a future with our family. We are not asking for anything extra or want special treatment.

As I grew up looking at Roots and other movies about slavery, it increased my respect for what our ancestors endured.

We have historically been beaten and unfairly treated, yet we continue to trust in a Jesus that America has painted as a white man. We know that He came to this earth as a man, but He is a Spirit.

More recently, with the biopic Just Mercy and the horrendous murder of George Floyd, it's so hard to believe that as a people, we have come so far, yet we are still trapped in an emotional/mental slavery of this world. When you watch the news, we hear this subliminal message to "Stay in your lane, you are beneath us, you will never succeed because of the color of your skin." This is what we hear loud and clear: "You don't have the ability to think for yourself or have the notion to be innovative."

What resilient groups of people African Americans, Native Americans, and Jews are. Like the children of Israel, God is always with us, no matter what we go through. Evil and racism will always exist until Jesus comes back, despite His dying on the cross and reconciling all men (and women) unto Himself. Yet we know that we wrestle not against flesh and blood. The media plays it out as Whites versus Blacks, Democrats versus Republicans, and us versus them. However, distractions from the enemy manipulate our emotions in a charged climate to engage us in strife. One final thought:

> Genesis 1:27
> So, God created man in His own image. He created them male and female.

Bruh James

J ames is the author of the book of the Bible named after himself. He challenges believers that call themselves followers of Christ to act like real ones. However, James was not a part of his brother's earthly ministry. He became a believer in Jesus after His resurrection. I wonder:

> Was there a reluctance to see Jesus, his brother, as the risen Savior?

> Did he view Jesus as the brother who abandoned the family business?

> Did he believe that "G" was just doing His thang and He would return home?

> Did James not like to travel?

> Did Mary not want her baby to travel with his bro?

> Did Jesus not invite James to be one of His disciples on purpose?

> Was James not as "spiritual" as the twelve?

I don't know the answer to any of these questions. Nevertheless, James understood the assignment and went hard for Jesus as His servant. Do you see your siblings or other family members serving Christ? What is your hesitation to follow Jesus? Is it Jesus or your family member? Are you harboring past family hurt or childhood sibling rivalry? COVID, mass shootings, and rumors of war have shown us more than ever that tomorrow is not promised and now is the time.

Many people know that Jesus exists but believe they simply have time or don't want to give up having so much aspects of fun.

> James 4:13–14 (CSB)
> Come now, you who say, Today or tomorrow
> we will travel to such and such a city and
> spend a year there and do business and make
> a profit. Yet you do not know what tomorrow
> will bring-what your life will be! For you
> are like a vapor that appears for a little while
> then vanishes.

This verse is not to shame you or make you feel afraid. It's the truth. Having truth allows you to make an informed decision. Love your family while you can. Forgive your family while you can. Serve God while you can.

The Wheels on the Car Go Round and Round

Psalm 34:7
The angel of the Lord encamps around those
who fear Him and rescues them.

A s a former preschool teacher, you always have your go-to
songs to gain a sense of control and peace. "The Wheels on the Bus" is one of my favorite songs because it is upbeat and interactive. However, it's interesting when the words of a song play out in your own life.

In 2011, shortly after having lunch with my "new" husband, I was heading back to work in the Churchill area of Richmond, Virginia. As I was approaching the red light, I was ending my phone call after receiving my confirmation for making a payment. Suddenly, I was thrust forward. A GRTC Caravan hit me. The one passenger onboard told the police that I had been on my cell phone and had backed up into the caravan. As a result of her statement, I received a ticket and had to go to court. The police officer apologized for giving me a ticket, and I told him it was okay because he was just doing his job. However, I told him I was not worried because Jesus saw it all. Three days later, I received a call from my insurance company that the GRTC Caravan had cameras on it, and it showed he indeed had hit me.

February 2014, my eleven-year-old daughter asked me to take her to school because she believed she would miss the bus, looking for a particular shirt. I loaded up her ten-month-old brother and his diaper bag. I decided to drop him off last to daycare. After she got out of the car in the front of the school, I proceeded to enter the two-lane road leading from school. I saw the bus my daughter was supposed to be on approach me. I said to myself, "This bus is too close and is going to hit me." I gripped the stirring wheel as I put the car in park. That bus grazed the driver's side of my Dodge Avenger. Then I had an "epiphany"—My baby is in the back seat! The good thing was he was in an infant rear-facing seat in the middle of the backseat. He was fine, and I was just a little shaken. Even though the kids on the bus stated that the bus driver had hit me, conveniently, her cameras were not working.

A few days after Christmas in 2019, I was parking in front of the State Social Services downtown. I put my hazard lights on and retrieved my package of background checks. I told the security officer, who I needed to see, to expediate these forms for my foster parents. After the call was made, I turned around to take a seat in the lobby. To my surprise, I saw my Pilot moving slowing down the street. "Oh my God, someone is stealing my car!" I ran to the door and saw the car rolling slowly through the green light. Then I realized my car was not stolen, but I had not put it in park. The Lord had allowed the car not to hit another car or person. It reminded me of Denzel Washington as an angel in The Preacher's Wife blowing (wind) to make Whitney Houston's character bump into her husband Courtney B. Vance. I jumped in the car as it slowly rolled to the curb of the next street. No one was in the car, and I began to cry. But was there someone in the car?

In every incident above, the angels of the Lord were all around. These encounters have caused me to pause and to not take life for granted. I thank God for His protection every day.

Trust Issues

Proverbs 3:5–6 (CSB)
Trust in the Lord with all your heart. And do
not rely on your own understanding. In all
your ways know him, and He will make your
paths straight.

There are very few people in my life whom I don't trust. And in not trusting people, that tends to reflect my mistrust of Christ at times. We are quick to quote, "You have not because you ask not!" Well, I have asked plenty of times and had no doubt that it would work in my favor. Sometimes, it didn't. I stood in faith for three who I just knew would be healed and continued to encourage other women. I had recently taken a divine healing class at church. I had a new foundation and understanding of what Jesus did on the cross for our sins, illness, and mental health. My eyes were wide open to the context for the scriptures in Isaiah 55 and could really apply it now.

I honestly believed for my mother-in-law, First Lady Gilliam, and Dr. Lois Evans (Tony Evans's wife). Even though I never met Mrs. Evans, I was truly blessed by her ministry to mothers and pastors' wives. I had faith, and I saw these women recover and keep on living for Christ. They all went to heaven. There is comfort knowing without a doubt they are in the arms of the Lord. However, there is no time limit on grief when you lose loved ones, even though I know that they are not actually lost.

This is the part of my faith that I struggle the with most: when I pray and believe the Scriptures in an unwavering manner and yet the opposite happens. In these incidences, I must believe that God's will trumps my preference. I have to rely on His sovereignty and know He is looking at not just today, tomorrow, but eternity.

Treasures

Matthew 6:21 (NIV)
For where your treasure is, there will your
heart be also.

If someone was to visit my very first apartment, they would assume I did not live alone. Despite all the "stuff," it was just me. Everything has a story behind it or an event. It could be a Christmas gift or a bargain I just could not resist. In the passage from Matthew, Jesus reminds me that I cannot take these things to heaven. During this Lenten season, I must remember that He is all I really need—my Main Source. It's important for me to seek first the kingdom (Matt. 6:33), and all that other stuff will be added unto me as well.

Hidden in His Shadow

Psalm 91:1 (NIV)
Whoever dwells in the shelter of the Most
High will rest in the shadow of the Almighty.

S hadows are historically known to provide early evidence
that light travels in straight lines. I am not sure about that,
but I know that God is omnipresent. He is everywhere at the
same time.

Shadows represent God's protection, presence, and rescue
from danger. Moses composed the ninety-first psalm as he was
ascending into the clouds hovering over Mount Sinai. He was
reassuring himself of the Almighty's protection from the angel
of destruction. Sounds like the original self-talk to me. Verse 14
says, "I will protect him because he knows my name." Wow!

There have been times in my life when I know that Jesus
was protecting me. It was not always from physical harm. There
was a time that we could not afford to get my car repaired to
pass inspection. My mother drove this particular car and was
afraid to drive around with an expired inspection sticker. So,
we switched cars. There were times I had to drive right past the
police station to get to work, but He hid me.

Years ago, I had to provide my license number so my prospective employer could run my driving records. Everything came back fine. However, I learned a few weeks later that there was a lapse in my insurance, and it did not show up.

My daughter had a balance on her tuition account. We wanted to apply for some scholarships, but they wanted her official transcripts. Usually, there is hold on your account until the balance is zero. However, when the business office checked, there was no hold.

I am not for one minute promoting being unethical or lying. I believe when God sees your motives to be pure and you are trying your best, He hides you.

Don't Co-Sign Sin

Y ou know when you are doing wrong. Instead of admitting that we are powerless to avoid sin without God, we continue in our own strength and fail. We sin and feel justified because of what other people do, or we say, "I could be doing worse." We know better! Well, the saying goes, "We do better when we know better"—right? Not when you view it as knowledge or information that does not have the ability to impact your life. Romans 12:2 says that we are transformed by the renewing of our minds. In order to be renewed, my mind must go through a continual process of being restored, refreshed, and replenished. You gain a sense of spiritual strength. You reset your thoughts to be the opposite of the world's view. That is not conforming even when it seems very easy to do. When we transform, we no longer look like ourselves. You know; it's like a robot that transforms into a car—totally unrecognizable from our previous selves. This is a process of casting down thoughts that exhort themselves against God's work. Even if we struggle to understand or believe it for ourselves, we must trust God's work. In essence, I do better when I let the wisdom of God empower me to change. Change takes time, but we must want to change.

Who's Your Daddy?

Philippians 2:3–4
Do nothing out of selfish ambition or vain
conceit. Rather, in humility value others above
yourselves, not looking to your own interests
but each of you to the interests of the others.

O ne day I went to the Exxon station near my apartment
to get some gas. I was single at the time and tried to get
gas during the daytime. I went inside to pay for my gas and
to get something to drink. The cashier read my license plates
GZUSKID. He was openly gay and had no shame about it.
When asked about the meaning of my plates, I simply explained
I was a child of God, a daughter of Jesus, so to say. He said
he did not know Jesus had any kids. I replied, "Well, He does
now." A few weeks passed by before I headed back to same gas
station. This time, I used my debit card at the pump because of
the rain. I swiped it twice, but it would not go through. I had
just got paid, so I had money. On the third time, it went through,
and I drove off after filling up.

About a month later, I was back at this same gas station.
I went inside, and the same cashier was working. He told me
he had seen me weeks ago trying to get gas outside in the
rain. He said his co-worker was going to call the police on me
because she thought I was trying to steal gas. He said, "I told

her GZUSKID would not steal gas!" He said he flipped the switch so I could get some gas. Would he have done that if I was rude to him or beat him down with scriptures? Just because we don't agree with someone's lifestyle does not mean we can't be kind and show God's love.

Jesus and Jacks

John 10:27–29
My Sheep hear my voice, I know them, and they follow me, I give them eternal life, and they will never perish. No one will snatch them out of my hand. My father, who has given them to me, is greater than all. No one is able to snatch them out of the Father's hand.

You remember playing jacks when you were a kid? The first few times you bounced the ball and picked up jacks was easy. Once you started getting into the higher numbers, it was hard to gather so many jacks scattered far from each other. You had to scoop up all the jacks and get the ball in one swift scoop.

This image came to mind one day while reading a devotional from *Jesus Calling* by Sarah Young as I focused on the part about how no one can snatch them (me) out of His hand. There have been many times I have struggled to see God's hand in a situation, especially when I have already prayed. No matter how far we separate our lives from His Word or ignore His presence, He has the ability grab us out of our mess and put us back on the right path. Proverbs 3:5–6 says, "And He will direct our paths."

The word *snatch* makes me think deeper about the thief and what is being "taken." No one snatches anything that is rightly belongs to them. Oftentimes when someone snatches something out of someone's hands:

1. The person gets mad at the owner.
2. The thief needs to get away.
3. What is being snatched has great value.

> John 10:10 states, "The thief comes to kill, steal, and destroy." As God's children, we have targets on our backs. Of course, Satan is mad at God because we have chosen to serve Him and not jump ship. Although, there are times our decisions and actions mirror the world. The mere fact that the devil tries to snatch us out of God's hand helps me understand and not underestimate our value to the kingdom of God.

Does Heaven Have a Back Door?

John 14:6
Jesus told him, "I am the way, the truth and
the life. No one comes to the father except
through me."

I have been to more funerals than I care to count. I attended
funerals that both my grandmothers ushered, and I had no
idea who had passed away or what a funeral was. When I gave
my life to Christ in college, I started to understand the concepts
of heaven and eternal life.

Christians' funerals are homegoing celebrations. It's a time
to laugh and reflect on memories. Of course, we will miss them,
and we will grieve, but not forever. The book of Thessalonians
assures us that the "dead in Christ" shall rise first. They are all
sleeping. Their bodies are in the ground, but their spirits are
with the Lord.

Have you ever been to a funeral and question if the person
did not know the Lord? You know, when people struggle to
say nice things about the person, they make very general and
vague statements like, "He was a good man" or "She loved
her children." But what about their souls? Well, if the saints
go marching in those pearly gates, where is the back door
for the others? Is there a side door they can slide in? I have

been to several people's funerals, especially family, and their relationship with the Lord is suspect. These are some of the conversations I have with my husband as he has officiated funerals and weddings.

My mentor from college Sandra Thornton would say, "You don't have to judge people, but you can be a fruit inspector." Our feelings are different for the elderly person who was gravely ill over the person who died because of violence, COVID, or drugs. Our emotions are all over the place. Yet a life is a life, all precious in the eyes of the Lord, and we need to learn to feel the same.

When we walk around people, the love and light of Christ grows to pull them directly to Him. We can no longer take for granted that coworkers and family members know Christ. Yes, one minute they are quoting scriptures on Facebook, then the next they are cursing on TikTok. They are confused, thinking that's okay. We were at one time also thinking we could proclaim Jesus one minute and live any kind of ungodly way while bringing Him glory. However, at some point, we need to check in and ask if they know Christ. Sometimes we have made up in our mind they don't want to hear what we have to say, or we fear rejection. What if they ask us a question we can't explain, or they put us on blast in front of others we may know?

However, if we think of the rich man who was in Hades who wanted someone to warn his five brothers not to end up in a place of torment like him, time is winding up, and Jesus is returning sooner than we think. Get ahold of your feelings and close the back door.

Lessons from a Father

Psalm 133:1 (NIV)
How good and pleasant it is when God's
people live in harmony.

O n February 18, 2023, I had the extreme honor of eulogizing my dad, Mr. Willie Mack Patterson. Although his passing was unforeseen, I believe he did his best to prepare me and my sisters the best he knew how. The above scripture reflects the day of my father's funeral. In other translations, it says brothers dwell in peace. Everyone in attendance, whether family or friends, was there in unity/love/peace celebrating the life of my daddy. It was beautiful to see the genuine love and support of this unexpected event for the Patterson family had just laid to rest their oldest brother six months prior. As the oldest child out of five (three girls and two boys) I wanted to convey the five essential things he taught me.

1. Love of words—My dad always talked to me like I was older. He used "big" words to explain things to me as a child. He was thinking outside of the box and on a higher level. He taught me how to read fast, and he would ask me questions after I read things. Comprehension was big to him. I love the etymology, or the original meaning of words. I love how their meanings change

with culture and their ability to express emotions. I
enjoy writing poetry and devotionals. I have published
works and plan to do more.

2. Love of music—My dad loved music. He had those
old vinyl records and would turn up the volume. It was
nothing for him to play some Stevie Wonder, Diana
Ross, or Michael Jackson. He would be singing one
song and then start singing all the lyrics to "Your Grace
and Mercy." He would tell me that us young folks did
not know what good music was, and that was a mess
we listened to now. I love music also. At my last place
of employment, they referred to me as the DJ. Many
mornings you would pass my office and hear some
good ole gospel music. Later after lunch or a staff-
building event, you would hear '90s clean hip hop
music or R&B.

3. Unfiltered communication—My dad never bit his
tongue. He had no filter and honestly did not care if
he hurt your feelings. This sounds unempathetic, but
I believe he was freer than most of us oppressing our
feeling. I believe God gaveme opportunities to speak
in church on behalf of my grandmothers or at places
of employment under my supervisors' request. Public
speaking is natural like breathing for me. There were
years I feared rejection or that I would hurt someone's
feelings, so I kept the peace and my mouth shut.
However, I have learned over the years from my dad that
there is value is being honest and authentic with people.

4. Sense of humor—I used humor as a defense mechanism
as a child. If I thought you were going to put me on
blast or there was awkward tension in the air, I would

crack a joke. My dad had an uncanny wit that was quick and sometimes harsh. He once called my spaghetti "mess" because the sauce was mixed with pasta and meat. Unbeknownst to me, he wanted it all separate and prepared on demand. However, he requested the same spaghetti during my next visit. Once he told his new cardiologist that he was retired but that his occupation was that he was a Black man in America, and that was a job within itself.

5. Family oriented—My dad valued being with his family at social functions. Even though this changed as he got older regarding his siblings, he loved to see his children and hear his grandchildren laugh. He wanted all five of his children to visit him and have a spaghetti dinner. As people grew and found their own paths, we were adults at this point, stretched across four states, and ranging in age from forty-nine to twenty-five years. Yes, Papa was a rolling stone, and no grass grew under his feet. He was a proud "Pop Pop." He loved us, and we loved him right back, even if it was hard at times.

For the most part I had a decent relationship with my father. Of course, there were times that it went through typical transitions and boundary settings. However, I will always honor and cherish the memory of my father. I am thankful my children had a chance to spend time with him.

Part 3: Poetry

Black Love

Press

The battle is given to those who endure to the end.

Lord, I'm tired; I swear I can't make it until then.

Life is tough, and I feel so alone.

Paying bills and facing trials, I hate being grown.

Lord, in Your Word You said you'll never leave me.

I ain't too proud to beg Lord, I need Thee.

To order my steps and help me run this race.

Sometimes I feel beat down so, I slow my pace.

Like Paul, I must forget things
which are behind and reach forward?

Press toward the goal for the prize of the call upward!

Make Love Last

Nothing last forever, but you can make love last.

You must do the work.

Like a moth to flame or rocket those blasts,

Keep each other first after God in that order.

Pray over your family and nurture your daughter.

November 7th is a day that you'll always remember.

The two become one, a perfect, united member.

Black Light

How can two walk together unless the two agree?

Can dark and light even dwell in unity?

I am made in my Father's image; He created me.

A chocolate hue is a reflection of the Trinity.

I am Black, and I am light

I embody God's love and His with all my might.

Am I an oxymoron—can I be Black and light?

The things people say about Black folks make you wanna fight.

God does not make mistakes, and He doesn't waste time with junk.

Don't let the devil or circumstances keep you in a funk!

God knew you in your mother's womb,

And He'll help guide your days.

Remember you are fearfully and wonderfully made.

So, yes, you too are Black and light.

Shine bright like a diamond and take flight.

The Ultimate Gift

Be sure to give honor where honor is due.
To our pastor who strategically prayed us through.

All those difficult times and very challenging seasons
When the devil told us to give up, so many reasons.

God's ultimate gift besides His Son to the church is pastors.
They give us hope, imitate Christ, and help us endure.

Today we celebrate a mortal man and servant Pastor Gilliam,
Doing warfare in the kingdom and putting the flesh in the
mausoleum.

We thank you for boldly approaching the throne on our behalf
We gladly follow your leadership like Moses with his staff.

You teach the Word with such fire, and you are not
ashamed of the gospel. God's vision and call on your life is
supernaturally fulfilled.

We are one body, one people, one mind, and one faith.
Union Hope and Pastor Gilliam, let's carry on and run
this race.

Black Love

Country boy, good heart, and a cheesy grin,
He's a confident leader and my favorite friend.
My husband kisses my face when the sun rises up.
He makes me laugh before it goes down.
He's the butter to my beans and the sweet to my potato.
He's the ice to my tea and the container for my stewed tomatoes.
He's my everything and everything I am not.
At the same time, he can make me so mad and hot.
He's the gift the Father granted me
To love and never forsake faithfully.
I know that I love Him and trust Him with my heart.
Today, Calvin Brown, let's never forget to recharge like at the
start. Happily ever after can exist in real life.
It's a perpetual state of forgiveness and ignoring strife
Intended for the devil to divide homes and marriages.
With God in the middle, we can bear it.
Every day because His mercies are made new to His
No matter what, God's alive, so there's no reason to fuss.

A Legacy of Love

A three-strand cord is not so easily broken with God in
the middle.
Marriage is not a token.
That's the only way a couple can truly survive.
Fifty years of holy matrimony with periodic vows revived.
Two walking together,
and deciding to agree.
Amos would be the first to says that's not so easy.
Two people from different paths
yet one heart regenerates.
Today we take time out with the Caseys to celebrate.
A genuine love of two who
met when they were young.
They weathered life's storms and
even had some fun.
So, here's to the next fifty years unless the Lord shall tarry.
Walking unified and growing in grace is their itinerary.

Mom

We do not have the best relationship in the world,
But I love you.
I wish I knew when it all went downhill.
But I love you.
I want us to have a mother–daughter bond
But I love you.
Some healing must take place.
But I love you.
When I look in the mirror, I see a little girl Longing and
looking for your approval.
But I love you.
I know I am not perfect and have Said some things to upset you,
But I love you.
We cannot change the past, but
We can move forward.
But I love you.
Let us hit the reset button and start over But I love you.
I forgive you and hope you forgive me.

Love Is a Verb

Love is the verb you show me every day.
When you kiss me every morning goodbye and come home
after work to stay.
It's easy to love from afar.
The image of my face remains when I leave in the car.
You chose to love me unconditionally despite my flaws and
immaturity.
Each year our unity grows stronger, although it's hard to
recognize at times
The devil knows God's awesome plan for our lives, ministry,
and family.
He seeks daily to demise.
Thank you for making a better effort to speak my
love language. Our quality times and acts of kindness
have doubled.
God has given our marriage mileage.
I know our past may haunt us like crimes. Forgetting
what is behind, I look forward to being with you for an
indefinite lifetime.

Fifty Shades of Brown

This month we celebrate Black history,

The struggle of our people and their victories.

There are people who want us to be ashamed of our color.

But when they look below the surface, they will discover

That we are more alike than different, and Black is beautiful.

We are unique, we have style, and that's indisputable.

Then the Lord took the brown dust of the earth, and He formed man, not delayed.

I am fearfully and wonderfully made unto the image of God.

If I am a true reflection of my Father, then I must be "fly."

I am your chestnut, cocoa butter, -your caramel chew and beige boo.

Like the Shulamite woman, I am dark but lovely

I am your hot chocolate, pecan pie, mocha latte, and brown sugar baby.

My beauty is not from my locs or gray contacts or even the way I am stacked.

God sees my heart and gentle spirit more than my outward appearance; that's a fact.

Whether BBQ or fried, God used a brotha's rib to form a sistah.

Black folks let's recognize that each one of us is precious in the Lord's eyes.

Our time on earth is limited, so get busy because time flies.

Let's uplift, encourage, and exalt one another.

When it comes down to it, all we got is each other.

Black Power

J.B. said it loud,
"I'm Black, and I'm proud!"

But if Martin, Malcolm, and Nelson were alive, would
they be wowed?
Yes, as African Americans, we have made great strides.
In research, medicine, and sports, our ancestors smile with pride.
There was a time in the past when we had to use the outhouse.
And not too long ago, we had some folks in the White House.
Yet violence, hate, and self-degradation are happening all
over the land.
When I look at my children, I'm
uncertain about their future, man.
Grandma said we have a God who sits high and looks low.
His Holy Spirit dwells in us and lets our "soul glow."
Just like Daryl Jenkins in
the Coming to America movie,
We got people building walls preventing.
travel across the sea.
What will it take to make America great again?
You missed or deleted the text Without Jesus, you won't win.
I mean, I believe America is great, but we can do better.
Look at the dollar bill and don't be a forgetter.
It says, "In God we trust!" Our resilient forefathers did.

Nowadays, we just pray for more and struggle to fit it under the lid.

If this earth is not my home but I have to stay for a while,

If each one teaches one but we don't stretch beyond our home and church yard,

Sharing the gospel being a positive role model will be hard.

I am a Christian, Black, and woman, all three.

Accepting my identity comes from Christ, that's why He died on the tree.

Can I rep Christ, be sassy, and support my race?

Have I got it twisted and lost my place?

As a people, we need to act like the kings and queens we were created to be.

Taking authority, dominion, and destroying stereotypes and walking in victory.

Jumpstart My Heart

Contrary to popular belief, I don't always have it going on.
I'm cool, wear fresh clothes, and sound smooth on the phone.
But deep down inside, this dude dealing with some stuff.
No one would agree; they think I'm tough.
Life has knocked me down, causing my heart to skip a beat.
I try to get back up, but I can't. I feel so weak.
Pain, drama, and despair are all around,
Feels like an anchor is pulling me down.
She stepped on the scene and made her presence known.
Our friendship in a short time has truly grown.
She encourages me to fulfill God's will.
She challenges me, and through my body, she sends a chill.
Her opinion is appreciated, even when we don't agree.
She helps me to think positively and not focus on me.
I got strength now, feel like I can run this race.
With her by my side, we'll speed up the pace.

Happy Mother's and Father's Day to You

You are Mom. You are the reason I am who I am.

Because you love me. I can never repay you for all your sacrifices over the years. You are my breath in my body. You are the heart that beats in my chest.

You are my very soul. I am everything with you and nothing without you. I love you more than you can ever know. Thank you for loving me first.

Happy Father's Day to you, Mom. To the one who raised me. You stood in the gap when no one else would. I love you, Mom; you're my hero.

About the Author

 Born and raised in Portsmouth, Virginia, she is a proud graduate of Virginia Commonwealth University with a bachelor's in psychology and a minor in religious studies. She holds an associate degree in early childhood education from Reynolds Community College. She has a diploma in biblical studies from Faith Landmarks Bible Institute. She has always had a love for children, books, and God. She enjoyed reading books as a kid. She won essay contests in middle and high school that later morphed into poetry during college. Now she enjoys using her gifts to tell distinctive stories and write devotionals. She is a wife, mother of three, and grandmother of two. She has been a CPR/first aid instructor since 2005 and an election official for the city of Richmond since 2012. She became an election chief in 2020. She has the pleasure of sitting on a few early childhood boards and has taught on the community college level. She resides in Henrico, Virginia. She is a co-author of *Words of Wisdom Volume II*. She is excited to publish her first book with her brother as illustrator.

Facebook: Cybil Brown
LinkedIn: Cybil Brown

Email:
2r1browns@gmail.com
Website: 2r1brown.com

Von Bashay Faulks

A Virginia native. Woodrow Wilson High School graduate class of '95. Attended Art Institute of Fort Lauderdale in Florida and has a family-first focus on life. Enjoys watching sports, spending time with family, and all things art related. Education is the key to unlocking a bright future.

Printed in the USA
CPSIA information can be obtained
at www.ICGtesting.com
CBHW051116050924
14101CB00045B/726